GOO

MODELING

FOR STRATEGY & ANALYSIS

Build clear, structured models
for better business decisions

ONRAMP ANALYTICS

ISBN: 9798319421005

First Edition

TABLE OF CONTENTS

Introduction

Learning how to build models can be incredibly valuable for assessing and analyzing different aspects of a business. By bringing together raw data and assumptions, models can generate insights and outputs that support business decisions and strategic thinking.

This book isn't about building full financial statements; it's about structure, logic, and clarity when building a Google Sheets model. Whether you're modeling customer behavior, inventory, or revenue, the same core principles apply.

Throughout the guide, we will provide numerous examples and visuals to illustrate the concepts we cover. We've also included a comprehensive case study that appears throughout the book to demonstrate how each component of a model comes together in practice. You can download this case study as an Excel file using the link below, which can be imported directly into a blank Google Sheets file (File > Import):

https://onrampanalytics.com/quickfit-case-study/

This book will cover seven key components of a Model:

1. **Raw Data:** Internal or external data that serves as a reference and should not be edited directly. This includes information like historical sales data, which provides the foundation for the rest of the model.

2. **Calculations:** Logic, scratch work, or analysis used to manipulate data, test ideas, or support other parts of the model. This includes data analysis that can define an assumption or refine raw data.

3. **Assumptions:** Inputs such as growth rates, prices, customer churn, or market share. Assumptions may also introduce structural groupings, like segmenting products by region or category, to align data with the model's purpose.

4. **Model:** The structure that connects everything together. It uses raw data, assumptions, and calculations to produce meaningful results.

5. **Output:** High-level summaries or visuals that communicate the model's results in a clear and concise format.

6. **Scenarios**: Multiple alternative cases to test how changes in assumptions or inputs affect a model's outcome.

7. **Key**: Area at the beginning of the model that defines what type of formatting is used and describes the role of each sheet.

Regardless of the complexity and granularity of a model, the goal is to generate output that summarizes key information and is based on a set of assumptions. These outputs help guide strategic planning, assess direction, and inform other key actions.

As illustrated in the image below, the output of a simple revenue model provides a high-level summary of both historical and forecasted revenue for a business, broken down by product, product segment, and region.

Revenue Summary
In $ millions

Revenue by Product	Historicals				Forecast				CAGRs		
Product	2021	2022	2023	2024	2025	2026	2027	2028	21-24	24-28	Notes/Sources
Smartwatch	31	32	34	38	41	45	49	53	8%	8%	
Smart Glasses	16	18	19	22	24	26	28	30	10%	8%	
Portable Air Purifier	14	14	15	18	19	20	21	22	9%	5%	
Solar Backpack	10	10	11	13	14	15	15	16	10%	4%	
Smart Sleep Mask	10	11	12	14	15	16	17	18	13%	5%	
Total	**81**	**84**	**91**	**106**	**113**	**120**	**129**	**138**	**9%**	**7%**	

Revenue by Segment	Historicals				Forecast				CAGRs	
Segment	2021	2022	2023	2024	2025	2026	2027	2028	21-24	24-28
Smart Tech	47	50	53	60	65	70	77	83	9%	8%
Personal Wellness	24	25	27	32	34	36	38	39	11%	5%
Outdoor & Adventure	10	10	11	13	14	15	15	16	10%	4%
Total	**81**	**84**	**91**	**106**	**113**	**120**	**129**	**138**	**9%**	**7%**

Revenue by Region	Historicals				Forecast				CAGRs	
Region	2021	2022	2023	2024	2025	2026	2027	2028	21-24	24-28
North	17	18	18	22	24	25	27	29	10%	7%
West	16	17	19	21	23	24	26	28	10%	7%
South	15	16	17	20	21	22	24	26	9%	7%
East	33	33	37	43	45	48	52	55	9%	7%
Total	**81**	**84**	**91**	**106**	**113**	**120**	**129**	**138**	**9%**	**7%**

While the underlying data and information can be much more detailed, aggregating this information into a structured summary helps highlight macro-level trends that can inform a business decision.

Section 1:

Raw Data

Explanation

Raw data serves as the **starting point of a model**, representing the original, untouched inputs before any manipulation or analysis.

This can include:

- **Internal data** such as sales records, customer transactions, or product-level performance

- **External data** like market benchmarks, industry trends, or competitor reports

Why It Matters

Raw data gives the model both credibility and structure, serving as the basis for all assumptions, calculations, and projections. If the raw data is messy or incomplete, the model's output won't be reliable.

To maintain accuracy and traceability:

- Do **not** edit raw data directly.

- Make any refinements or adjustments to raw data in the *Calculations* section instead.

Let's say we're building a revenue forecast. An example of raw data would be information that includes product-level revenue by year, broken down by region. A well-structured raw data table might have these columns:

- **Product ID**: A unique identifier for each product

- **Product Name**: The item's name

- **Region**: Where the product was sold

- **Yearly Revenue**: Annual revenue for each product/region/year

Office Revenue

In $ thousands

Prod_ID	Product_Name	Region	2021	2022	2023	2024	Notes/Sources
PA92342	Desk	EMEA	7.1	7.8	7.5	8.9	*Office Revenue (ERP)*
PA19231	Chair	EMEA	3.5	4.2	3.9	4.8	
PA77210	Cabinet	EMEA	2.3	2.7	2.5	3.2	
PA83903	Bookcase	EMEA	1.9	1.7	2.0	2.4	
PA10332	Table	EMEA	1.8	2.1	2.4	2.9	
PA04932	Shelf	EMEA	6.0	6.9	6.2	7.5	
PA92342	Desk	APAC	2.4	2.8	3.2	4.0	
PA19231	Chair	APAC	2.5	2.5	2.4	3.1	
PA77210	Cabinet	APAC	1.6	1.8	2.0	2.0	
PA83903	Bookcase	APAC	1.9	1.7	2.1	2.5	
PA10332	Table	APAC	6.5	6.2	6.8	7.8	
PA04932	Shelf	APAC	3.1	3.5	3.3	3.9	
PA92342	Desk	RoW	2.4	2.3	2.8	3.0	
PA19231	Chair	RoW	1.7	1.9	1.8	2.2	
PA77210	Cabinet	RoW	1.6	2.0	2.3	2.7	
PA83903	Bookcase	RoW	7.0	7.7	7.4	8.5	
PA10332	Table	RoW	3.3	3.1	3.8	4.6	
PA04932	Shelf	RoW	2.4	2.6	3.0	3.4	

This format keeps the data easy to read, filter, and reference. It also enables the use of formulas like XLOOKUP or SUMIFS, which are especially useful in modeling.

Note: The only acceptable additions to a raw data sheet are:

- A **header** (e.g., "Office Revenue") to clarify the sheet's purpose

- **Notes/Sources** placed off to the right of the table

These additions help users understand where the data came from and how it fits into the overall model.

Business Case Example

QuickFit Solutions is a mid-sized company that sells a variety of consumer products designed to enhance daily life through technology and convenience. They cater to business professionals, families and tech-savvy consumers, offering products through two main channels:

- **Online direct sales**

- **Retail store sales**

QuickFit's five core products are:

1. Smartwatch
2. Smart Glasses
3. Portable Air Purifier
4. Solar Backpack
5. Smart Sleep Mask

To evaluate performance and support strategic planning, we will build a model **to forecast revenue over the next four years**. The goal is to determine which products and regions warrant a larger share of investment and marketing dollars.

Step 1: Gather Historical Data

We have collected two key data files to serve as the foundation for the model:

- **Online Historical Sales** (2021-2024)

- **Retail Sales** (2021-2024)

These files include annual revenue data by product and region, and will act as our raw data for the model.

Step 2: Organizing Raw Data in Google Sheets

We will start by opening a new Google Sheets file and renaming the first sheet to **Raw Data >>**.

This sheet will function as a **reference sheet** to organize our *Raw Data* section. Rather than storing data directly here, we will use it to label and reference where our raw data sheets are located.

Raw Data >> ▼

Next, we will create two sheets to the right of this:

- **Online Historical Sales**

- **Retail Historical Sales**

Raw Data >> ▾   Online Historical Sales ▾   Retail Historical Sales ▾

Each sheet should contain the actual data for its respective channel. Color all three sheets **dark gray** to indicate they are part of the *Raw Data* section.

Step 3: Verify Raw Data Setup

Here is what the model should look like at this stage:

- **Raw Data >>**

- **Online Historical Sales**

- **Retail Historical Sales**

Raw Data >> ▾   Online Historical Sales ▾   Retail Historical Sales ▾

Within the **Online Historical Sales** sheet, we have the following information:

Online Historical Sales

In $ millions

Prod_ID	Product_Name	Region	2021	2022	2023	2024	*Notes/Sources*
TD98420	Smartwatch	West	4.5	5.2	6.1	5.9	*Online Sales (ERP)*
TD29432	Smart Glasses	West	3.8	3.6	4.5	5.2	
TD92943	Portable Air Purifier	West	3.2	3.5	3.3	4.0	
TD88239	Solar Backpack	West	2.4	2.2	2.8	3.3	
TD02311	Smart Sleep Mask	West	2.3	2.5	2.4	3.0	
TD98420	Smartwatch	East	5.7	5.4	6.5	7.3	
TD29432	Smart Glasses	East	2.6	3.1	3.6	3.4	
TD92943	Portable Air Purifier	East	3.4	3.1	3.7	4.2	
TD88239	Solar Backpack	East	2.2	2.4	2.1	2.8	
TD02311	Smart Sleep Mask	East	2.4	2.2	2.6	3.1	

Within the **Retail Historical Sales** sheet, we have the following information:

Retail Historical Sales

In $ millions

Prod_ID	Product_Name	Region	2021	2022	2023	2024	Notes/Sources
TD98420	Smartwatch	North	7.1	7.8	7.5	8.9	*Retail Sales (Bookings)*
TD29432	Smart Glasses	North	3.5	4.2	3.9	4.8	
TD92943	Portable Air Purifier	North	2.3	2.7	2.5	3.2	
TD88239	Solar Backpack	North	1.9	1.7	2.0	2.4	
TD02311	Smart Sleep Mask	North	1.8	2.1	2.4	2.9	
TD98420	Smartwatch	South	6.5	6.2	6.8	7.8	
TD29432	Smart Glasses	South	3.1	3.5	3.3	3.9	
TD92943	Portable Air Purifier	South	2.4	2.3	2.8	3.0	
TD88239	Solar Backpack	South	1.7	1.9	1.8	2.2	
TD02311	Smart Sleep Mask	South	1.6	2.0	2.3	2.7	
TD98420	Smartwatch	East	7.0	7.7	7.4	8.5	
TD29432	Smart Glasses	East	3.3	3.1	3.8	4.6	
TD92943	Portable Air Purifier	East	2.4	2.6	3.0	3.4	
TD88239	Solar Backpack	East	1.9	1.7	2.0	2.5	
TD02311	Smart Sleep Mask	East	2.0	1.9	2.2	2.8	

At this stage, our raw data is correctly inserted, structured, and labeled.

Note: Before moving to the next section, check the raw data for missing values, duplicate entries, or inconsistencies. Any adjustments should be made in the *Calculations* section to preserve the source data.

Section 2:

Calculations

Explanation

The *Calculations* section is where all intermediate work takes place. This includes cleaning, transforming, and preparing data before it becomes a finalized assumption or flows into the model. Keeping this section separate improves transparency and makes auditing easier for users.

How it Differs from Raw Data and Assumptions

Unlike raw data, which should remain untouched, and assumptions, which contain finalized model inputs, the *Calculations* section serves as a **workspace**.

Emphasizing this separation strengthens the model's integrity:

- **Raw Data** is imported but should not be edited.

- **Calculations** include any data transformations.

- **Assumptions** contain only clean, finalized inputs used by the model.

What Belongs Here

Analysis that would be done in the *Calculations* section include:

- Averaging market data to derive an input

- Weighting multiple benchmarks to create a blended rate

- Cleaning and reshaping inputs (e.g., converting months to years)

Example: Estimating COGs using External Data

Here's a scenario where the *Calculations* section plays a key role: estimating cost of goods sold (COGS) for a new product using external market data.

Suppose a company plans to launch a new product next year. With no internal or factory-level data available yet, they've gathered COGS figures for similar competitor products from a market research provider, **XYZ Research.**

To estimate the COGS for this new product, the company would:

1. Import the external COGS data into a new sheet.

2. Calculate an average COGS value based on that data.

3. Feed that average into the *Assumptions* section as the cost input for the new product.

New Product COGs

COGs by Competitor Product					
Products	**DM**	**DL**	**Other**	**Total**	*Notes/Sources*
Product #1	$12.67	$2.00	$3.12	$17.79	*XYZ Research*
Product #2	$11.83	$1.80	$2.73	$16.36	
Product #3	$10.92	$2.40	$1.88	$15.20	
Product #4	$12.33	$3.50	$1.73	$17.56	
Product #5	$11.74	$2.00	$2.34	$16.08	
Avg. COGS	$11.90	$2.34	$2.36	$16.60	

While this example is relatively simple, more complex models might involve additional variables, such as adjusting for currency, regional factors, or revenue normalization. The key is that all data manipulations used to transform or derive inputs from external sources should occur in the *Calculations* section, not in the *Raw Data* section or the *Assumptions* section.

This structure keeps the model clean and easy to follow. It ensures that assumptions are clearly separated from the underlying analysis that supports them, making the model more transparent and easier to update.

Business Case Example

Building on our QuickFit case, we've identified a need to incorporate external data from a market research provider, **ABC Tech Research**, to support one of our growth assumptions.

In this model, we won't forecast revenue at the individual product level. Instead, we've grouped the five products into broader product segments to simplify the analysis.

For example, **Smartwatch** and **Smart Glasses** are grouped into a segment called **Smart Tech**, as they share similar market drivers such as wearable technology adoption and digital integration trends. The remaining products are grouped similarly, each into their own strategic segment.

Using segments allows us to apply unified growth assumptions to product groups with shared characteristics, resulting in a more streamlined model that is easier to maintain.

Because the Smart Tech growth rate requires multiple steps, all supporting work will be handled in the *Calculations* section.

Step 1: Google Sheets Setup

1. Create a new sheet labeled **Calculations >>**. This will serve as a reference sheet.

2. To the right of it, add a new sheet labeled **Tech Market Growth.**

3. Color both sheets green to visually group them.

Calculations >> ▾   Tech Market Growth ▾

Your file should now include:

- **Calculations >>**

- **Tech Market Growth**

Step 2: Import External Growth Rates

In the **Tech Market Growth** sheet, we've imported projected growth rates for several industry drivers relevant to QuickFit's Smart Tech products. These projections span four years (2025–2028).

Tech Market Growth

Tech Market Yearly Growth by Industry Driver

Tech Industry Drivers	2025	2026	2027	2028	Notes/Source
Tech Adoption Rate (General)	8.3%	7.6%	9.3%	8.1%	*ABC Tech Research*
Wearable Technology Adoption	10.1%	9.8%	11.1%	10.4%	
Augmented Reality (AR) Advancements	12.5%	13.1%	11.7%	12.0%	
Virtual Reality (VR) Growth	15.2%	16.1%	14.6%	15.7%	
3D Printing Market Growth	7.3%	7.0%	7.5%	7.1%	
Quantum Computing Progress	9.1%	8.9%	9.2%	9.6%	
E-commerce Growth	6.9%	6.8%	6.9%	6.6%	
Consumer Electronics Growth	5.8%	5.6%	5.7%	5.8%	
Social Media Platform Growth	4.9%	5.2%	5.0%	5.1%	

Step 3: Identify Key Industry Drivers

After reviewing the relevant tech industry drivers, we've determined that there are three key drivers we want to include in our calculation:

- **Tech Adoption Rate (General)**

- **Wearable Technology Adoption**

- **Consumer Electronics Growth**

Step 4: Assign Weightings

Each of the three drivers is assigned a weighting to reflect its expected influence on the Smart Tech segment:

- Tech Adoption Rate: 45%

- Wearable Technology: 30%

- Consumer Electronics: 25%

Weighting

Tech Adoption Rate (General)	45%	45%	45%	45%
Wearable Technology Adoption	30%	30%	30%	30%
Consumer Electronics Growth	25%	25%	25%	25%

These weightings allow us to blend the three growth rates based on relevance and priority.

Step 5: Calculate the Blended Growth Rate

Now, we multiply each growth rate by its corresponding weighting, then sum the results to calculate the final **blended growth rate** for each year.

Weighting				
Tech Adoption Rate (General)	45%	45%	45%	45%
Wearable Technology Adoption	30%	30%	30%	30%
Consumer Electronics Growth	25%	25%	25%	25%
Smart Tech	8.2%	7.8%	9.0%	8.2%

These blended growth rates will later be referenced in the *Assumptions* section to inform the forecasted growth for the **Smart Tech** product segment.

Section 3:

Assumptions

Explanation

The *Assumptions* section contains the key inputs that drive the model's logic and results. These are values that reflect future expectations, strategic decisions, or estimates that are not found directly in the raw data.

Unlike raw data, which should remain untouched, and calculations, which may involve complex analyses, **assumptions are clean, finalized inputs** that flow directly into the model. Think of assumptions as the core levers that define how your model will behave.

What Belongs Here

Common types of assumptions include:

- **Growth rates** (e.g., product segment revenue growth)
- **Pricing assumptions**
- **Volume drivers** (e.g., number of units, site visitors)
- **Churn or conversion rates**
- **Timing inputs** (e.g., launch dates, contract periods)
- **Segment groupings** that introduce new ways of organizing information in the model

Example 1: Regional Segmentation

Let's say we want to analyze performance differences across coastal and non-coastal states, but our raw data does not have this classification. We can create a segmentation table to accomplish this:

Coastal Segmentation

Coastal Assumptions		
States	**Coastal Tagging**	*Notes/Sources*
California	Coastal	
Colorado	Non-coastal	
Florida	Coastal	
Ohio	Non-coastal	
Iowa	Non-coastal	

This assumption table groups existing state-level data into a new classification that doesn't appear in the original raw dataset. By assigning each state a **Coastal** or **Non-Coastal** label, the model can generate insights along this new dimension which is something that is not possible with the raw data alone.

Because this classification is subjective and manually created, it belongs in the *Assumptions* section, not in the *Raw Data* section.

However, simply creating the table isn't enough. To be useful, the segmentation must be **linked to the model** using an existing field such as **State** from the raw data.

Example 2: Revenue Growth by Region

Another common type of assumption table involves including forecasted growth rates for specific segments, such as by region or state:

Revenue Growth by State

Revenue Assumptions						
States	**2025**	**2026**	**2027**	**2028**	**2029**	*Notes/Sources*
CA	2%	5%	5%	4%	4%	
CO	8%	7%	7%	6%	6%	
FL	4%	4%	3%	5%	8%	
OH	6%	5%	5%	5%	4%	
IA	1%	2%	2%	1%	1%	

This type of table makes it easy to:

- Apply localized growth assumptions across different segmentations

- Maintain a structured format for updates and scenario planning

Business Case Example

In this section, we'll define the finalized inputs that will drive the model's revenue forecast. Specifically, we'll:

1. Group QuickFit's five products into meaningful **segments**.

2. Assign a **growth rate** to each segment over a four-year forecast period (2025-2028).

These assumptions are entered into two separate sheets:

- A **Product Segmentation** table that maps each product to a segment

- An **Annual Revenue Growth** table that defines the growth assumptions for each segment

These are structural decisions that don't exist in the raw data. Instead, they reflect how we choose to analyze and segment the business. Like earlier examples, these assumptions are entered cleanly, without complex calculations and logic, so they remain easy to audit and update.

Step 1: Google Sheets Setup

1. Create a new sheet labeled **Assumptions >>**.

2. To the right of that, create a new sheet labeled **Product Segmentation**.

3. To the right of that, create a sheet labeled **Annual Revenue Growth**.

4. Color all three sheets blue to visually group them as part of the *Assumptions* section.

Assumptions >> ▾   Product Segmentation ▾   Annual Revenue Growth ▾

Your file should now include:

- **Assumptions >>**
- **Product Segmentation**
- **Annual Revenue Growth**

Step 2: Define Product Segmentation

The first assumption table we'll create is the **Product Segmentation** table. This table groups QuickFit's products into strategic segments that reflect the target market and product usage.

Below is the product segmentation table, with products on the left and their corresponding product segment assumptions on the right:

Product Segmentation

Product Assumptions		
Products	**Product Segment**	*Notes/Sources*
Smartwatch	Smart Tech	
Smart Glasses	Smart Tech	
Portable Air Purifier	Personal Wellness	
Solar Backpack	Outdoor & Adventure	
Smart Sleep Mask	Personal Wellness	

Organizing products into segments allows us to apply assumptions more consistently across similar items. This simplifies the model and makes it easier to incorporate market-level insights.

Step 3: Define Revenue Growth Rates

In the **Annual Revenue Growth** sheet, we'll enter the expected growth rate for each product segment across the next four years:

Annual Revenue Growth

Revenue Growth by Segment					
Segment	**2025**	**2026**	**2027**	**2028**	*Notes/Sources*
Smart Tech	8.2%	7.8%	9.0%	8.2%	
Personal Wellness	4.8%	5.3%	6.1%	4.5%	
Outdoor & Adventure	5.5%	4.9%	3.2%	4.0%	

These growth rates will be applied to historical revenue for each product segment, enabling us to forecast future revenue performance.

Note: The Smart Tech growth rates reference the **Tech Market Growth** sheet created earlier in the *Calculations* section. Because these values come from another sheet, they are colored **green**.

Section 4:

Model

Explanation

The *Model* section is where everything you have organized so far begins to take shape. It serves as the logical framework that connects raw data and assumptions to produce meaningful insights, such as forecasts or projections that inform business decisions.

This section is where the actual mechanics of the model live. Whether the goal is to forecast revenue, simulate user behavior, or calculate inventory levels, this is where structured formulas are used to translate inputs and raw data into meaningful insights.

To build a model, we'll often use **unique identifiers** to connect information across multiple sources. A unique identifier is any value that consistently exists across datasets, such as product IDs, employee names, regions, or customer types. These identifiers serve as the link between raw data, assumptions, and the model's core logic.

Example: Simple Revenue Forecast

Let's say we're building a revenue model and have two raw data sources with historical revenue for different regions. We want to consolidate this data in the *Model* section:

Raw Dataset #1

in $ millions

Prod_ID	2017	2018	2019	2020	*Notes/Sources*
ZF8432	12.5	15.1	18.3	22.0	*Source #1*
ZF2904	7.9	6.8	6.2	5.5	
ZF9849	6.0	7.2	8.9	10.3	
ZF2043	13.2	12.5	11.8	11.0	
ZF4029	4.1	5.0	6.3	7.7	
ZF9204	19.5	18.7	17.4	16.2	
ZF7382	11.3	13.0	15.6	18.4	
ZF3204	6.7	7.3	7.9	8.6	

Raw Dataset #2

in $ millions

Prod_ID	2017	2018	2019	2020	Notes/Sources
ZF8432	10.2	12.5	15.1	18.3	*Source #2*
ZF2904	8.4	7.9	6.8	6.2	
ZF9849	5.1	6.0	7.2	8.9	
ZF2043	14.0	13.2	12.5	11.8	
ZF4029	3.5	4.1	5.0	6.3	
ZF9204	20.0	19.5	18.7	17.4	
ZF7382	9.8	11.3	13.0	15.6	
ZF3204	6.2	6.7	7.3	7.9	

To do this, we'll use the shared **Prod_ID** field as our unique identifier. Since this field exists in both raw data tables, we can copy the Prod_IDs into a new sheet in the *Model* section labeled **Revenue Forecast**. We'll also add column headers for each year (e.g., 2017-2020) to prepare for our consolidation.

Revenue Forecast

in $ millions

Revenue by Product ID					
Prod_ID	2017	2018	2019	2020	Notes/Sources
ZF8432					
ZF2904					
ZF9849					
ZF2043					
ZF4029					
ZF9204					
ZF7382					
ZF3204					

To combine the data, we can use SUMIFS to pull revenue from both sources based on the **Prod_ID**.

Revenue Forecast

in $ millions

Revenue by Product ID					
Prod_ID	**2017**	**2018**	**2019**	**2020**	*Notes/Sources*
ZF8432	22.8	27.7	33.4	40.3	
ZF2904	16.4	14.8	13.0	11.7	
ZF9849	11.2	13.3	16.1	19.2	
ZF2043	27.3	25.8	24.3	22.8	
ZF4029	7.7	9.2	11.3	14.0	
ZF9204	39.6	38.3	36.1	33.6	
ZF7382	21.2	24.4	28.6	34.0	
ZF3204	13.0	14.1	15.2	16.5	

Once the historical data is consolidated, we can layer in assumptions to project future revenue.

For example, let's say we have a separate table in the *Assumptions* section that lists each **Prod_ID** alongside its corresponding growth rate for the next three years.

Annual Revenue Growth

Revenue Growth by Prod ID			
Prod_ID	**2021**	**2022**	**2023**	*Notes/Sources*
ZF8432	8%	11%	6%	
ZF2904	12%	8%	10%	
ZF9849	6%	9%	11%	
ZF2043	9%	7%	7%	
ZF4029	8%	12%	10%	
ZF9204	10%	9%	9%	
ZF7382	6%	12%	8%	
ZF3204	9%	10%	13%	

Because the assumption table and the data in the **Revenue Forecast** sheet share the same Prod_IDs, we can connect them using a lookup formula.

In the **Revenue Forecast** sheet we'll:

1. Add columns for forecast years (e.g., 2021-2023).

2. In the first forecast cell, reference the final historical year's value.

3. Multiply that value by 1 plus the appropriate growth rate based on the matching Prod_ID from the assumptions table.

4. Lock the reference to the Prod_ID column so it stays fixed when copying the formula across.

5. Copy the formula across all rows and columns for the forecast years. Since the forecast years are aligned between the Revenue Forecast and Assumptions sheets, there's no need to adjust column references.

Revenue Forecast

in $ millions

Revenue by Product ID								
Prod_ID	2017	2018	2019	2020	2021	2022	2023	*Notes/Sources*
ZF8432	22.8	27.7	33.4	40.3	43.5	48.3	51.2	
ZF2904	16.4	14.8	13.0	11.7	13.1	14.2	15.6	
ZF9849	11.2	13.3	16.1	19.2	20.4	22.2	24.6	
ZF2043	27.3	25.8	24.3	22.8	24.9	26.6	28.5	
ZF4029	7.7	9.2	11.3	14.0	15.1	16.9	18.6	
ZF9204	39.6	38.3	36.1	33.6	37.0	40.3	43.9	
ZF7382	21.2	24.4	28.6	34.0	36.0	40.4	43.6	
ZF3204	13.0	14.1	15.2	16.5	18.0	19.8	22.2	

Once complete, this table represents the model. It combines raw data and assumptions using structured, traceable formulas to generate insights.

Business Case Example

With product segments and growth assumptions defined for QuickFit, we're now ready to build the *Model* section. This is where we'll combine the historical revenue with our assumptions to calculate projected revenue.

The goal of this section is to:

- Pull in historical data

- Layer in product segmentation assumptions

- Apply growth rates to product segments to calculate forecasted revenue

Step 1: Google Sheets Setup

1. Create a new sheet labeled **Model >>**.

2. To the right of that, add a sheet labeled **Revenue Forecast**.

3. Color both sheets black to visually identify them as part of the *Model* section.

Your file should now include:

- **Model >>**

- **Revenue Forecast**

Model >> ▾   Revenue Forecast ▾

Step 2: Linking Raw Data Using Product ID

To begin building the model, we need to consolidate our two raw data sources: **Online Historical Sales** and **Retail Historical Sales**. These sheets contain revenue by product but are separated by sales channel.

To combine them, we'll use the **Product ID** as our unique identifier since it exists in both sheets. In the **Revenue Forecast** sheet, we'll:

1. Copy all Product IDs from the Online Historical Sales sheet and paste them into the **Revenue Forecast** sheet.

2. Copy all Product IDs from the Retail Historical Sales sheet and paste them directly under the first list of Product IDs.

3. Remove duplicate IDs. To do this, select all of the IDs and go to **Data > Data cleanup > Remove duplicates**.

This leaves us with one unique list of Product IDs, which will serve as the foundation of our model.

Prod_ID
TD98420
TD29432
TD92943
TD88239
TD02311

Step 3: Bringing in Product Names

Next, we'll bring in the **Product Name** for each Product ID. This improves readability and will be necessary when we map product segments.

To do this, we'll use a lookup formula such as **XLOOKUP** to pull the product names from one of the historical sales sheets. If a product appears in only one dataset, we'll adjust the formula accordingly.

Prod_ID	Product_Name
TD98420	Smartwatch
TD29432	Smart Glasses
TD92943	Portable Air Purifier
TD88239	Solar Backpack
TD02311	Smart Sleep Mask

Step 4: Referencing Product Segmentation

Now that we have both Product ID and Product Name in place, we can pull in the Product Segment using the **Product Segmentation** sheet. Once again, we'll use a lookup formula to match the product name to its assigned segment.

This step is critical, as our growth assumptions are applied at the product segment level.

Prod_ID	Product_Name	Product Segment
TD98420	Smartwatch	Smart Tech
TD29432	Smart Glasses	Smart Tech
TD92943	Portable Air Purifier	Personal Wellness
TD88239	Solar Backpack	Outdoor & Adventure
TD02311	Smart Sleep Mask	Personal Wellness

Step 5: Adding Region

To allow for regional revenue forecasting, we'll expand our list of products to include every product-region combination. We'll:

1. Duplicate the Product ID / Name / Segment block three additional times (to create four sets total).

2. Add a **Region** column and assign the regional value North, South, East, or West to each block.

This sets up a matrix that allows us to model revenue by product and region.

Prod_ID	Product_Name	Product Segment	Region
TD98420	Smartwatch	Smart Tech	North
TD29432	Smart Glasses	Smart Tech	North
TD92943	Portable Air Purifier	Personal Wellness	North
TD88239	Solar Backpack	Outdoor & Adventure	North
TD02311	Smart Sleep Mask	Personal Wellness	North
TD98420	Smartwatch	Smart Tech	West
TD29432	Smart Glasses	Smart Tech	West
TD92943	Portable Air Purifier	Personal Wellness	West
TD88239	Solar Backpack	Outdoor & Adventure	West
TD02311	Smart Sleep Mask	Personal Wellness	West
TD98420	Smartwatch	Smart Tech	South
TD29432	Smart Glasses	Smart Tech	South
TD92943	Portable Air Purifier	Personal Wellness	South
TD88239	Solar Backpack	Outdoor & Adventure	South
TD02311	Smart Sleep Mask	Personal Wellness	South
TD98420	Smartwatch	Smart Tech	East
TD29432	Smart Glasses	Smart Tech	East
TD92943	Portable Air Purifier	Personal Wellness	East
TD88239	Solar Backpack	Outdoor & Adventure	East
TD02311	Smart Sleep Mask	Personal Wellness	East

Step 6: Pulling Historical Revenue Data

Before moving on, let's add headers, notes/sources, and relevant historical and forecast years to our model structure:

Revenue Forecast
in $ millions

Revenue by Product, Segment, and Region

Prod_ID	Product_Name	Product Segment	Region	2021	2022	2023	2024	2025	2026	2027	2028	Notes/Sources
TD98420	Smartwatch	Smart Tech	North									
TD29432	Smart Glasses	Smart Tech	North									
TD92943	Portable Air Purifier	Personal Wellness	North									
TD88239	Solar Backpack	Outdoor & Adventure	North									
TD02311	Smart Sleep Mask	Personal Wellness	North									
TD98420	Smartwatch	Smart Tech	West									
TD29432	Smart Glasses	Smart Tech	West									
TD92943	Portable Air Purifier	Personal Wellness	West									
TD88239	Solar Backpack	Outdoor & Adventure	West									
TD02311	Smart Sleep Mask	Personal Wellness	West									
TD98420	Smartwatch	Smart Tech	South									
TD29432	Smart Glasses	Smart Tech	South									
TD92943	Portable Air Purifier	Personal Wellness	South									
TD88239	Solar Backpack	Outdoor & Adventure	South									
TD02311	Smart Sleep Mask	Personal Wellness	South									
TD98420	Smartwatch	Smart Tech	East									
TD29432	Smart Glasses	Smart Tech	East									
TD92943	Portable Air Purifier	Personal Wellness	East									
TD88239	Solar Backpack	Outdoor & Adventure	East									
TD02311	Smart Sleep Mask	Personal Wellness	East									

Now we'll bring in historical revenue from 2021–2024 by referencing the **Online Historical Sales** and **Retail Historical Sales** sheets. Each product-region combination needs to pull revenue data from both sales channels.

To do this, we'll use the SUMIFS function with the following logic:

1. Use **Product ID** and **Region** as the criteria in the SUMIFS function.

2. Reference the appropriate **Year** column directly in each formula, based on the layout already structured in the model.

3. Lock cell references where appropriate.

4. Paste the formula across columns for 2021 through 2024, so each column pulls the value for its respective year.

This approach allows us to sum the revenue by Product ID and Region in each year. Once complete, we'll have a clean, consolidated view of historical revenue by product and region.

in $ millions

Prod_ID	Product_Name	Product Segment	Region	2021	2022	2023	2024	2025	2026	2027	2028	Notes/Sources
		Revenue by Product, Segment, and Region										
TD98420	Smartwatch	Smart Tech	North	7	8	8	9					
TD29432	Smart Glasses	Smart Tech	North	4	4	4	5					
TD92943	Portable Air Purifier	Personal Wellness	North	2	3	3	3					
TD88239	Solar Backpack	Outdoor & Adventure	North	2	2	2	2					
TD02311	Smart Sleep Mask	Personal Wellness	North	2	2	2	3					
TD98420	Smartwatch	Smart Tech	West	5	5	6	6					
TD29432	Smart Glasses	Smart Tech	West	4	4	4	5					
TD92943	Portable Air Purifier	Personal Wellness	West	3	4	3	4					
TD88239	Solar Backpack	Outdoor & Adventure	West	2	2	3	3					
TD02311	Smart Sleep Mask	Personal Wellness	West	2	3	2	3					
TD98420	Smartwatch	Smart Tech	South	7	6	7	8					
TD29432	Smart Glasses	Smart Tech	South	3	4	3	4					
TD92943	Portable Air Purifier	Personal Wellness	South	2	2	3	3					
TD88239	Solar Backpack	Outdoor & Adventure	South	2	2	2	2					
TD02311	Smart Sleep Mask	Personal Wellness	South	2	2	2	3					
TD98420	Smartwatch	Smart Tech	East	13	13	14	16					
TD29432	Smart Glasses	Smart Tech	East	6	6	7	8					
TD92943	Portable Air Purifier	Personal Wellness	East	6	6	7	8					
TD88239	Solar Backpack	Outdoor & Adventure	East	4	4	4	5					
TD02311	Smart Sleep Mask	Personal Wellness	East	4	4	5	6					

Step 7: Applying Growth Rates

Finally, we'll apply the growth rate assumptions from the **Annual Revenue Growth** sheet to forecast revenue.

1. In the first forecast year column (2025), reference the 2024 revenue value.

2. Multiply it by (1 + the 2025 growth rate) for the corresponding product segment.

3. Use a lookup formula (e.g., XLOOKUP) to pull the 2025 growth rate based on the product segment.

4. Lock references where appropriate.

5. Copy the formula across the forecast years.

Revenue Forecast

in $ millions

Revenue by Product, Segment, and Region												
Prod_ID	Product_Name	Product Segment	Region	2021	2022	2023	2024	2025	2026	2027	2028	*Notes/Sources*
TD98420	Smartwatch	Smart Tech	North	7	8	8	9	10	10	11	12	
TD29432	Smart Glasses	Smart Tech	North	4	4	4	5	5	6	6	7	
TD92943	Portable Air Purifier	Personal Wellness	North	2	3	3	3	3	4	4	4	
TD88239	Solar Backpack	Outdoor & Adventure	North	2	2	2	2	3	3	3	3	
TD02311	Smart Sleep Mask	Personal Wellness	North	2	2	2	3	3	3	3	4	
TD98420	Smartwatch	Smart Tech	West	5	5	6	6	6	7	7	8	
TD29432	Smart Glasses	Smart Tech	West	4	4	5	5	6	6	7	7	
TD92943	Portable Air Purifier	Personal Wellness	West	3	4	3	4	4	4	5	5	
TD88239	Solar Backpack	Outdoor & Adventure	West	2	2	3	3	3	4	4	4	
TD02311	Smart Sleep Mask	Personal Wellness	West	2	3	2	3	3	3	4	4	
TD98420	Smartwatch	Smart Tech	South	7	6	7	8	8	9	10	11	
TD29432	Smart Glasses	Smart Tech	South	3	4	3	4	4	5	5	5	
TD92943	Portable Air Purifier	Personal Wellness	South	2	2	3	3	3	3	4	4	
TD88239	Solar Backpack	Outdoor & Adventure	South	2	2	2	2	2	2	3	3	
TD02311	Smart Sleep Mask	Personal Wellness	South	2	2	2	3	3	3	3	3	
TD98420	Smartwatch	Smart Tech	East	13	13	14	16	17	18	20	22	
TD29432	Smart Glasses	Smart Tech	East	6	6	7	8	9	9	10	11	
TD92943	Portable Air Purifier	Personal Wellness	East	6	6	7	8	8	8	9	9	
TD88239	Solar Backpack	Outdoor & Adventure	East	4	4	4	5	6	6	6	6	
TD02311	Smart Sleep Mask	Personal Wellness	East	4	4	5	6	6	6	7	7	

Section 5:

Output

Explanation

The *Output* section is where the results of the model are summarized and presented. Its primary purpose is to present high-level data views that allow users to quickly extract meaningful insights.

While the detailed rows in a model such as revenue by product, region, or other crosscuts are important, they can often be difficult to interpret. The *Output* section helps distill that complexity into simple summaries that support faster, more informed decision-making.

Example: Summarizing Model Results

A revenue forecast might include hundreds of rows broken out by product, region, and channel. Instead of reviewing every line, we can summarize this detail to show total revenue by product or by region in a clean, digestible format.

Output

In $ thousands

Revenue by Product									CAGRs		
	Historicals				Forecast						
Product	2021	2022	2023	2024	2025	2026	2027	2028	21-24	24-28	Notes/Sources
Desk	72	79	86	95	101	112	126	140	10%	10%	
Chair	98	105	114	124	131	148	155	161	8%	7%	
Cabinet	73	80	88	93	98	110	112	124	8%	7%	
Bookcase	63	67	74	79	88	92	103	108	8%	8%	
Table	94	102	110	120	132	144	156	169	8%	9%	
Shelf	77	81	90	95	101	109	119	130	8%	8%	
Total	**478**	**513**	**563**	**606**	**652**	**713**	**770**	**831**	**8%**	**8%**	

Revenue by Region									CAGRs	
	Historicals				Forecast					
Region	2021	2022	2023	2024	2025	2026	2027	2028	21-24	24-28
APAC	196	211	232	247	265	293	316	338	8%	8%
EMEA	125	134	146	155	171	188	204	219	7%	9%
RoW	157	168	184	204	216	233	251	274	9%	8%
Total	**478**	**513**	**563**	**606**	**652**	**713**	**770**	**831**	**8%**	**8%**

<u>Note:</u> Keep outputs clean, visual, and focused on the metrics that matter most to a user.

Business Case Example

Now that we've calculated forecasted revenue for QuickFit by product and region, we can summarize the results to make it easier to interpret. While the model includes every product-region combination, this output will display total revenue broken out **individually** by product, segment, and region.

Step 1: Google Sheets Setup

1. Create a new sheet labeled **Output >>**.

2. To the right of that, add a sheet labeled **Revenue Summary**.

3. Color both sheets red to designate them as part of the *Output* section.

Your file should now include:

- **Output >>**

- **Revenue Summary**

Output >> ▾   Revenue Summary ▾

Step 2: Summarize Revenue by Product

We'll start by summarizing total revenue by product. This summary removes product segment and region details to focus on core product performance over time.

Using a SUMIFS formula, we'll pull this product-level data from the **Revenue Forecast** sheet to show both the historical and forecast revenue.

Revenue Summary
In $ millions

Revenue by Product									CAGRs		
	Historicals				Forecast						
Product	2021	2022	2023	2024	2025	2026	2027	2028	21-24	24-28	Notes/Sources
Smartwatch	31	32	34	38	41	45	49	53	8%	8%	
Smart Glasses	16	18	19	22	24	26	28	30	10%	8%	
Portable Air Purifier	14	14	15	18	19	20	21	22	9%	5%	
Solar Backpack	10	10	11	13	14	15	15	16	10%	4%	
Smart Sleep Mask	10	11	12	14	15	16	17	18	13%	5%	
Total	**81**	**84**	**91**	**106**	**113**	**120**	**129**	**138**	**9%**	**7%**	

Step 3: Summarize Revenue by Product

Next, we'll summarize revenue by product segment. We'll again use the SUMIFS function to total revenue for each product.

Revenue by Segment									CAGRs	
	Historicals				Forecast					
Segment	2021	2022	2023	2024	2025	2026	2027	2028	21-24	24-28
Smart Tech	47	50	53	60	65	70	77	83	9%	8%
Personal Wellness	24	25	27	32	34	36	38	39	11%	5%
Outdoor & Adventure	10	10	11	13	14	15	15	16	10%	4%
Total	81	84	91	106	113	120	129	138	9%	7%

Step 4: Summarize Revenue by Region

Finally, following a similar process that we used to create to the product and product segment output tables, we'll create a region-level output table.

Revenue by Region									CAGRs	
	Historicals				Forecast					
Region	2021	2022	2023	2024	2025	2026	2027	2028	21-24	24-28
North	17	18	18	22	24	25	27	29	10%	7%
West	16	17	19	21	23	24	26	28	10%	7%
South	15	16	17	20	21	22	24	26	9%	7%
East	33	33	37	43	45	48	52	55	9%	7%
Total	81	84	91	106	113	120	129	138	9%	7%

These summaries provide a high-level snapshot of QuickFit's revenue performance, giving users a clear and approachable view of the model's results. With this level of visibility, teams can make more confident decisions about where to focus marketing efforts and how to allocate investment dollars.

Section 6:

Scenarios

Explanation

Scenarios allow users to explore different potential outcomes by toggling between alternate assumptions or conditions in the model. While presented here as a separate section for clarity, scenarios are often integrated directly into the *Assumptions* section using dedicated scenario-specific inputs.

Scenarios are especially useful for stress testing, sensitivity analysis, and strategic planning. They help answer questions like:

- What if growth slows down next year?

- How would the business perform with higher churn?

- What happens if a new market performs better than expected?

In many cases, businesses build at least three types of scenarios:

1. **Base Case**: The expected or most likely outcome, grounded in current trends and historical data.

2. **Alternative Case(s)**: Variations that reflect different future conditions (e.g., economic downturns, aggressive growth, or unexpected shifts).

This structure allows model users to view how key model outputs shift under different assumptions, without altering the core logic of the model.

Example: Revenue Growth Scenarios

Below is a table showing forecasted growth rates under three different scenarios:

Revenue Growth Scenarios

Revenue Growth by Scenario					
Cases	2025	2026	2027	2028	*Notes/Sources*
Downturn Case	2.0%	2.3%	2.1%	1.3%	
Base Case	5.4%	6.2%	5.8%	3.7%	
Upside Case	8.0%	9.1%	8.6%	7.2%	

The table compares the **Base Case** with two alternate scenarios. For example, the **Downturn Case** uses lower growth assumptions to simulate slower economic conditions, while the **Upside Case** reflects a more optimistic view of future performance.

Business Case Example

To explore how assumptions affect the forecast, we'll build three growth scenarios in the QuickFit model: **Base Case**, **Downturn Case**, and **Upside Case**. Each scenario will contain its own set of growth assumptions and can be toggled within the model to view the resulting outputs.

Step 1: Google Sheets Setup

1. Navigate to the **Annual Revenue Growth** sheet.

2. Below the existing growth assumptions table, create three additional tables for **Base Case**, **Downturn Case** and **Upside Case**.

3. Label each table clearly.

Annual Revenue Growth

Revenue Growth by Segment					Notes/Sources
Segment	2025	2026	2027	2028	
Smart Tech	8.2%	7.8%	9.0%	8.2%	
Personal Wellness	4.8%	5.3%	6.1%	4.5%	
Outdoor & Adventure	5.5%	4.9%	3.2%	4.0%	

Base Case				
Segment	2025	2026	2027	2028
Smart Tech				
Personal Wellness				
Outdoor & Adventure				

Downturn Case				
Segment	2025	2026	2027	2028
Smart Tech				
Personal Wellness				
Outdoor & Adventure				

Upside Case				
Segment	2025	2026	2027	2028
Smart Tech				
Personal Wellness				
Outdoor & Adventure				

Step 2: Define Scenario Growth Rates

For each table, input the growth assumptions for each product segment. For example:

- **Base Case**: reflects expected performance

- **Downturn Case**: applies lower growth rates

- **Upside Case**: assumes stronger market performance

Each scenario should use the same product segments and structure. Only the growth rates should vary.

Base Case				
Segment	2025	2026	2027	2028
Smart Tech	8.2%	7.8%	9.0%	8.2%
Personal Wellness	4.8%	5.3%	6.1%	4.5%
Outdoor & Adventure	5.5%	4.9%	3.2%	4.0%

Downturn Case				
Segment	2025	2026	2027	2028
Smart Tech	3.5%	3.3%	3.9%	3.5%
Personal Wellness	3.0%	3.3%	3.8%	2.8%
Outdoor & Adventure	1.2%	1.0%	0.7%	0.8%

Upside Case				
Segment	2025	2026	2027	2028
Smart Tech	11.3%	10.7%	12.3%	11.3%
Personal Wellness	9.5%	10.5%	12.1%	8.9%
Outdoor & Adventure	6.6%	5.9%	3.8%	4.8%

Step 3: Dropdown Menu for Scenario Selection

In the **Annual Revenue Growth** sheet, create a dropdown menu labeled **Scenario**. Use Google Sheet's **Data Validation** feature to build a list with the following options: **Base Case, Downturn Case**, and **Upside Case**.

Scenario	Base Case

Step 4: Link the Selected Scenario to the Model

Once you've created the dropdown list in the **Annual Revenue Growth** sheet, we'll repurpose the top growth rate table to dynamically reflect the selected scenario.

To do this:

1. Use a formula like **XLOOKUP, CHOOSE**, or **IF** to reference the scenario selected in the dropdown menu.

2. In each cell of the top growth rate table, pull in the corresponding value from one of the three scenario tables below based on the selected scenario.

This setup allows the top table to act as a live reference for the model, automatically updating the growth rates based on the selected scenario. As a result, the model adjusts in real time without requiring any changes to its structural logic.

Our final **Annual Revenue Growth** sheet should look like this:

Annual Revenue Growth

Scenario	Base Case				

Revenue Growth Forecast by Segment					
Segment	**2025**	**2026**	**2027**	**2028**	*Notes/Sources*
Smart Tech	8.2%	7.8%	9.0%	8.2%	
Personal Wellness	4.8%	5.3%	6.1%	4.5%	
Outdoor & Adventure	5.5%	4.9%	3.2%	4.0%	

Base Case				
Segment	**2025**	**2026**	**2027**	**2028**
Smart Tech	8.2%	7.8%	9.0%	8.2%
Personal Wellness	4.8%	5.3%	6.1%	4.5%
Outdoor & Adventure	5.5%	4.9%	3.2%	4.0%

Downturn Case				
Segment	**2025**	**2026**	**2027**	**2028**
Smart Tech	3.5%	3.3%	3.9%	3.5%
Personal Wellness	3.0%	3.3%	3.8%	2.8%
Outdoor & Adventure	1.2%	1.0%	0.7%	0.8%

Upside Case				
Segment	**2025**	**2026**	**2027**	**2028**
Smart Tech	11.3%	10.7%	12.3%	11.3%
Personal Wellness	9.5%	10.5%	12.1%	8.9%
Outdoor & Adventure	6.6%	5.9%	3.8%	4.8%

Section 7:

Key

Explanation

The **Key** sheet is placed at the front of the model to help users quickly understand how the file is structured and how to interpret its content. It serves two main purposes:

1. It defines the formatting conventions used throughout the model such as color-coding to distinguish between inputs, formulas, and references.

2. It provides an **overview of each sheet**, summarizing the purpose of every section and helping users navigate the model efficiently.

Business Case Example

To support usability and transparency, we'll create **Key** sheet at the front of our model. This sheet defines the formatting conventions used and provides a reference for each sheet's purpose, structure, and how it connects to the rest of the model.

Step 1: Google Sheets Setup

1. Create a new sheet labeled **Key** and move it to the far left of the Google Sheets file.

2. Color the sheet **orange** to distinguish it from the rest of the model.

Key ▾

Step 2: Define Formatting Conventions

Next, in the **Key** sheet, we'll outline the formatting rules applied throughout the model. This includes color-coding conventions that indicate whether a value is a calculation, a hardcoded input, or a reference from another sheet.

Formatting	
Item	**Example**
Calculations	100
Hardcodes	100
References	100
Assumptions	100

Step 3: Define Sheet Structure

Below the formatting section, we'll include a table that lists each sheet name along with a brief description of its purpose (only include the description if the sheet is not a section divider).

Output >>	
Revenue Summary	Summary output of revenue by product, segment, & region
Model >>	
Revenue Forecast	Product by region historical and forecasted revenue
Assumptions >>	
Annual Revenue Growth	Revenue growth assumptions (2025-2028) for each product segment
Product Segmentation	Group products into product segments
Calculations >>	
Tech Market Growth	Smart Tech 'Base Case' assumption based off tech industry drivers
Raw Data >>	
Online Historical Sales	QuickFit online sales from 2021-2024
Retail Historical Sales	QuickFit retail store sales from 2021-2024

This layout ensures that any user can easily navigate the model structure and understand the purpose of each sheet.

Formatting & Styling

Explanation

Consistent formatting is a key part of building clear, professional models. Every styling choice in this book is intentional, aimed at making the model easy to read, maintain, and audit over time.

Font & General Styling

- **Font:** Garamond is used throughout the model and this book for its clean, readable, and professional look.

- **Font Size:** 11-point font is used consistently for readability.

Color Coding (Cells)

The model follows a clear color-coded font scheme that helps users understand what kind of input or reference they are looking at:

- **Black:** Used for standard formulas and calculations within the same sheet. It is also applied to static labels or raw data that should not be edited such as product names, IDs, regions, or any structural data used to organize the model.

- **Blue:** Represents hardcoded input values or assumptions. These are manually entered and are intended to be editable by the user. Blue cells typically include growth rates, price assumptions, conversion rates, and other inputs that drive the forecast.

- **Green:** Indicates values referencing another sheet or source. An example is using a lookup or conditional formula to bring in values from another section of a model. This makes it easy to trace dependencies and keep cross-tab logic transparent.

Table & Cell Formatting

- **Gridlines Removed:** Gridlines are turned off across all sheets for a cleaner layout.

- **Borders Under Headers:** Each table header includes a bottom border to clearly separate column titles from the data below.

- **Row Spacing:** Consistent spacing is applied between tables and rows to maintain a clean, uncluttered look.

Sheet Formatting & Structure

- **Sheet Naming:** Sheets are labeled clearly and consistently. Navigation indicators like ">>" (e.g., Assumptions >>, Calculations >>) are used to reinforce structure and flow.

- **Sheet Color Coding:**

  - **Raw Data:** Gray
  - **Calculations:** Green
  - **Assumptions:** Blue
  - **Model:** Black
  - **Output:** Red
  - **Key:** Orange

Assumptions

- **Cell Background Color:** Any direct assumptions in the model will have a blue background, indicating that the area contains user input.

- **Cell Font Color:** Hardcoded values are colored **blue**, while references to other sheets or sections such as the *Calculations* section are colored **green**.

Headers & Section Titles

- **Sheet Headers:** The sheet name is bolded and placed above each section, with a bottom border that extends across the data. This clearly defines the purpose of the sheet or section.

- **Data Tables:** Each data table includes a header row with a **black background** and **bold white text** to distinguish the table title from the data below.

By following these formatting principles, the model remains professional, consistent, and easy to work with, not only for the creator but for any teammate, client, or stakeholder who uses it.

Made in United States
Orlando, FL
19 July 2025

63101620R00040